"Dear Jesus ..."

"Greetings and kisses from your Antonietta..."

Written and Illustrated by

Sisters of Children of Mary

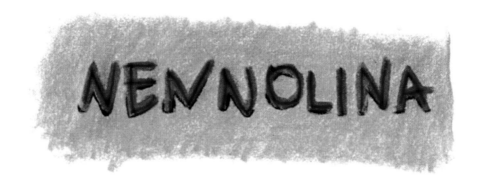

D1379214

"I thank you, Father, Lord of heaven and earth,
that you have hidden these things
from the wise and understanding and revealed them to infants;
yes, Father, for such was your gracious will."
-Luke 10:21

love for Love Publishing

5440 Moeller Ave
Cincinnati, OH 45212
www.childrenofmary.net

"Although she was a frail little girl, she managed to give a strong and vigorous Gospel witness…you can consider her a friend of yours, a model to inspire you. Her life, so simple and at the same time so important, shows that holiness is for all ages…Every season of our existence can be the right one for deciding to love Jesus seriously and to follow Him faithfully. In a few years, Nennolina reached the summit of Christian perfection that we are all called to climb; she quickly traveled the superhighway that leads to Jesus…Learn to know her and follow her example."

- Pope Benedict XVI

Antonietta 'Nennolina' Meo

December 15, 1930 – July 3, 1937

Dear Jesus,

I love you so much! I want to tell you again I love you so much! I give you my heart. Our dear Lady, you are so good, take my heart and carry it to Jesus."

– Antonietta

Dear Parents,

This book is intended to be a shared experience—you and your child pondering the inspirational writings of Venerable Antonietta Meo, who, although she died at the age of six, has been described as a mystic. Her letters to Jesus will help anyone of any age to grow in love for Our Lord Jesus in the Holy Eucharist!

Her love, although expressed with simplicity, takes us deep into Our Lord's Sacred and Eucharistic Heart.

Truly it will be time spent with your child

that you will treasure forever!

On December 15, 1930, ten days before Christmas in the great city of Rome, a beautiful little girl named Antonietta Meo was born. A great gift from God, her parents, Maria and Michele lovingly called her Nennolina.

Nennolina was a very joyful and lively girl who could always be found with a smile on her face. She loved to play, especially on the seashore, and like all little children she was a bit mischievous. However, Antonietta always wanted to be good, loving, and obedient especially towards her parents and teachers.   She brought joy to everyone around her and as a result she was loved by all.

Antonietta was a child just like the other children, but as the people who were close to her soon began to notice, there was something very special and extraordinary about this little girl.

God had placed many graces in the heart of Antonietta. These graces were preserved and nurtured in her heart because of the devout Catholic home in which she was raised. From a young age, Antonietta learned from her parents how to love God, the Blessed Mother, the saints, and the Holy Eucharist (also called the Most Blessed Sacrament) where Jesus is present Body, Blood, Soul, and Divinity.

At this time, Antonietta started school at the convent nursery. She loved school and the nuns who taught her. She would say,

"Dear Jesus I like school so much and I would be there also at night so in the morning I would be earlier at school and I would learn things more than the others ... and I want to study because I like it so much"

Dear Jesus, Today I want to be very good at school and not ever disobey the teacher. Greetings and Caresses from your child, Antonietta

Dear Jesus, today I got a grade of red and You forgive my sins.

Dear Jesus, today I got a grade of praiseworthy and I hope to get many of them because I want to become the first of the class to make you pleased ... and to make the teacher pleased, whom I wish well, but more I wish you well.

Out of all of her friends Jesus was her closest and best friend. Antonietta went to Church often to visit Jesus. She would kneel in front of the Tabernacle and talk to Him for a long time, telling Him beautiful things and invite Him to spend time with her.

Antonietta was always full of joy, because she was always thinking of Jesus. She kept Him close to her heart at all times, in the good and the bad. When she was 5 years old she got cancer in her bones. She had to have her left leg taken off because it got filled with the disease. It was very painful, but nothing, not even this disease, could take away her joy.

Dear Dad, I am very happy that Jesus has sent me this disaster you know ! ...At least I am the most beloved of Jesus.

Dear Jesus Eucharist, I wish you very well and I suffer this illness so that lots of souls will be saved and come into paradise to glorify you.

Dear Jesus Eucharist, I wish you so well !...Jesus I would like these three graces: The first, make me holy and this is the most important thing. The second give me souls. The third, make me walk well, truly this isn't very important. I don't say that you should give me back the leg, I gave you that!

The doctors gave her an artificial leg. It hurt and was uncomfortable for Antonietta, but she did not complain. Still filled with joy, she continued to visit Jesus, go to school, and play with her friends.

Dear Jesus Grown-up,
You know that today I got a 'praiseworthy' and also for a gift a notebook with the image of your Mommy, and also Sister Noemi gave me a bouquet of artificial flowers and an image of little St. Therese who was playing in the garden when she was little with her sister!..."

Dear Jesus...tomorrow I go back to school, for four days I have been on vacation, and I have done all the work that the teacher gave me to do. Greetings and kisses from your dear very affectionate, Antonietta

In the evenings, Antonietta studied catechism with her mother. She really enjoyed learning about God and His Church !

"I hope that soon I will be able to begin to learn catechism at school but then again already I know a good bit."

Nennolina's little heart would be filled with love every time she learned more about Jesus, our Eucharist. The love would flow like a waterfall out of her heart onto paper as she wrote letters to Jesus

Dear Jesus,
Yesterday evening I did not write You but this evening I will write you a beautiful long letter to tell you so many beautiful things and they really please You. Dear Child Jesus make me become good so that one day I can be with you in Paradise. Dear Jesus tell your mommy to help me to be good.

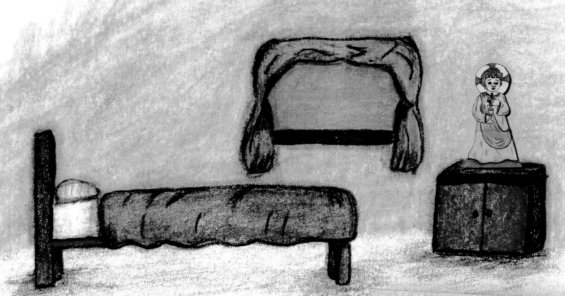

Every evening after Catechism, she placed her letters under the statue of Baby Jesus at the foot of her bed. She did this so Jesus could come and read them during the night while she slept.

Dear God the Father, tell Jesus that my heart hopes to be very beautiful...I know that Your dear son Jesus suffered so much but tell him that I want to make reparation for our sins, and I will make lots of sacrifices.

Dear God the Father, I wish You very very well today I am happy that I received confession but today I have been a little bad but tomorrow I promise You that I will be good at school at home with my sisters and especially I will be good for you.

Dear Jesus, my love for you is all. Jesus save your child from any danger. Give me souls...I give you my heart.

Antonietta started to write love letters to Jesus because she was preparing for the most important day of her life: her First Holy Communion.

"Most Dear God the Father! I am very glad that Your Son Jesus is coming into my heart . . . Dear God the Father tell Jesus that I am very happy to receive him and tell him also that when I will write to Him He will hear in all the little letters that I want Him."

Dear Jesus, I would like Holy Christmas to come soon and always I tell You because I desire it a lot and You will read it in all the letters that I want to receive you soon...Dear Jesus who knows how happy I will be that day when You will come into my heart and I believe that You will be happy too.

Dear Jesus... Tomorrow I will write You a beautiful letter and also to the Madonnina

On Christmas day little Antonietta was going to receive Jesus into her heart for the very first time. She was over-joyed ! She was counting down the days, the hours, the minutes, until Christmas. She did this not because of any toys she might get, but because Jesus was going to come into her heart in Holy Communion.

That was ALL she wanted !

She loved Him SO MUCH !

"O Child Jesus I have been waiting for You for so long in my heart ! I can't wait for it to be Christmas! It is true that Christmas is the most beautiful day! It is beautiful because I want to receive You into my heart."

Dear Jesus who knows how beautiful will be that day of Holy Christmas when I will receive you for the first time and I will be very happy and hope to make many sacrifices because I want to make you a beautiful room in my little heart all full of flowers and of lilies and a nice bed to keep you warm warm, and tightly tightly to my heart

As
the days,
the hours,
the minutes

went by;

Antonietta's

letters kept

piling up !

Dear God the Father, make me become always more good so that I can receive your dear Son more worthily.

Dear Jesus, who knows when that blessed day of Holy Christmas will come to be able to receive you in my little heart, but great in love.

Dear Jesus come soon since it is so long that my heart is waiting for you.

Dear Jesus, only 19 days are lacking and then I will receive You into my heart

Dear Child Jesus, I will prepare you a beautiful soft soft little crib dear Jesus.

Dear Child Jesus...It will be beautiful that night when I will come to receive you just when you will be born and my heart will be happy, happy, happy.

Dear Jesus who knows how happy I will be when you will come into my heart and I believe that you will be happy too

Dear Jesus how beautiful that night will be when I will receive you in my little heart, because it will be the first time that I will receive you.

Dear Jesus Eucharist, I know that 9 days are lacking what beauty !

Dear Jesus Eucharist, I hope that Holy Christmas can come soon, Dear Jesus I wish you so well, I am very very happy to receive you into my heart, Dear Jesus, when I am older I would like to be a nun to be your spouse. Are you happy Jesus that I might become your spouse? Caresses greetings and kisses from Your Antonietta

Dear Jesus, tell God the Father that I thank him and I thank you also and also the Holy Spirit because in a little bit it will be Holy Christmas.

Madonnina You are good. Descend upon us and bless us. Take my heart and bring it to Jesus. Oh Madonnina, you are the star of our hearts

Dear Jesus, I am already so tranquil, glad and happy that You are coming into my little heart but great in love.

Most dear Jesus Eucharist...if you only knew how happy I am! ...Only one day more and then I will receive You into my heart dear Jesus! Dear Jesus ! I will ask You for many graces and now I will tell all, first I will adore You and will thank You then will ask You for the things needed....

Dear Jesus Eucharist

I am very happy that in a few hours I will receive You in Holy Communion.
Dear Jesus tell God the Father that I thank Him, You and the Holy Spirit because in a few hours I will receive You in Holy Eucharist and I will be very very glad!!
Dear Jesus I love you very very very much...
Dear Jesus tell the Madonnina that I want to receive You from her hands,
Dear Jesus help the Church, the Pope, the Clergy, my parents, me, and the world.

Come. Come oh my Jesus to your Antonietta and Jesus

The moment finally arrived !

It was midnight on Christmas Day, December 25, 1937.

Antonietta was now 6 years old.

The joy she felt in her heart could not be contained!

She was finally going to receive her sweet Jesus.

After months and months of preparing her heart, Jesus was more than just a close friend; He was her *EVERYTHING*, and now He was finally going to come into her heart!

"Dear Jesus I love You a lot. Dear Jesus, I want to do what You want, I want to abandon myself into Your Hands . . . Dear Jesus tell the Holy Spirit to illuminate me and fill me with His Grace and bless me. Dear Jesus tell the Madonnina to bless me and that I want to remain always under her mantle and pray to You so that You give me the graces necessary to my soul and my body. Dear Jesus I want to abandon myself into Your Hands and make me what You want. I want to repeat that I love You a lot, really a lot."

Antonietta put on her white dress and entered the Church. The white dress was simply a visible sign of her soul which she had made *"white white"* for Jesus.

During Mass, Antonietta remained very still. She watched and listened attentively to everything that the priest said and did.

When the moment of consecration came, the whole Church was in complete stillness and silence-- except for the low voice of the priest as he spoke the words of consecration. Antonietta remembered those words, because they are the very same words that Jesus spoke at the Last Supper:

"This is My Body...This is My Blood."

Antonietta knew well what happens at every Mass as she fondly recalled all that the nuns taught her. She learned that the great miracle that takes place is called *transubstantiation,* which is when the bread and wine is changed into the Body and Blood of

Jesus. At that moment Jesus comes down from Heaven and is present on the altar in all His Glory !

The long awaited moment finally came. . . . . . .

Antonietta walked slowly and quietly up to the Communion rail and knelt down. She remembered learning that Jesus is present completely in each and every little Particle of the Host, and that one does not want even the tiniest Particle to fall to the ground and be stepped on, because it would be Jesus Who would fall and be stepped on. How much this would hurt His Sacred Heart! Antonietta did not want that to happen to Jesus, so as she knelt to receive Communion she remained as reverent and still as she could as the priest placed Jesus on her tongue.

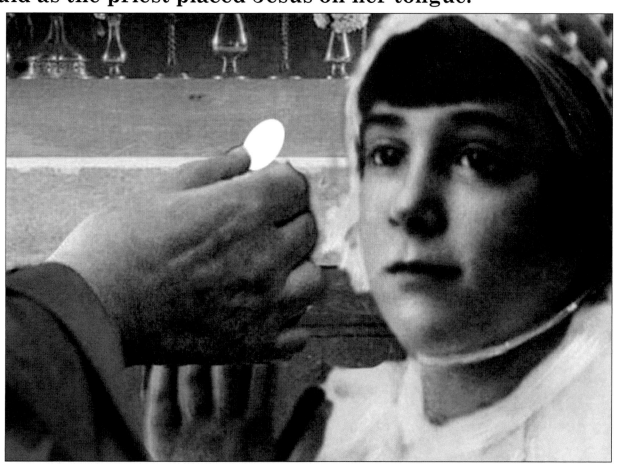

Her little heart overflowed with joy and love as Jesus, her Everything, was placed on her tongue. Jesus entered into her heart and there He remained, sharing with her the secrets of His Love. Her soul and His Soul were now one. Jesus was present within her physically in all His Glory and Divinity, and there He would remain substantially for about 15 minutes. This was the most important time in her life, so Antonietta spent not just 15 minutes but over an hour in prayer and thanksgiving.

"Dear Jesus Eucharist, I am so very, very happy that you have come into my heart. Never leave my heart. Stay forever and ever with me. Jesus, I love You so, I want to let myself go into Your arms and do what You will with me..."

Dear Jesus I want to be always enclosed in Your Heart, I want to be always with you. Dear Jesus I send you many greetings and kisses from Your Antonietta

Dear Jesus Eucharist,
I wish you very very well dear Jesus!...I know that You suffered a lot , and I want to go every Sunday to Mass where the sacrifice of the cross is renewed and where You make a sacrifice still greater in enclosing yourself in the Most Holy Sacrament of the altar. Dear Jesus I will come to receive you every Sunday, but I would like to receive you every day, but mom does not bring me. ...I greet you, I adore You oh Jesus!...and I want to be always on Calvary beneath the Cross.

Antoniettta and Jesus

Dear Jesus I know that they commit so many offenses against You, I want to make reparation for these offenses...I would enclose you inside of a house and you would not hear the offenses that are committed against You, so You could do this, come into my heart and remain closed with me and I will make many sacrifices for You and will tell You a few things to console You.

Despite the pain in her leg, Antonietta did not move, and her hands were joined in prayer as she paid attention to and talked to no one but Jesus. She did not want to waste a single second of those precious moments ! Jesus told her of His Love and she told Him of her love and many beautiful things as a friend talks to a friend.

"Dear Jesus I kiss you on your wounds and I adore You and I am Your dear Antonietta. Sacred Heart of Jesus I love you, Sacred Heart of Jesus Your Kingdom come."

Dear Jesus I am so happy to be your lamp and your Lily. The lamp that is the little flame of love, the lily which is the purity of the soul and both are on the altar to adore you, on the altar there is a beautiful flower which is me who adore you. These two things always keep you company like the lamp that burns day and night, so also the lily wants to be there to adore you always always.

This great love and desire that Antonietta had for Jesus did not end after her First Holy Communion. Each time she received Holy Communion and spent time with Jesus in prayer, her love for Him grew all the more.

"Do you like this music? Don't you hear little birds singing?" - Antonietta

Dear Jesus Eucharist ...when you return into my heart in the Holy Eucharist, put your grace into the wardrobe of my soul made of sacrifices and leave it always there

"Dear Jesus Eucharist my heart is bursting with love for you and I'm glad to receive You tomorrow morning in the Holy Communion..."

She was like a little bird soaring through the clouds towards Heaven. There she would sing, like little birds do, her ceaseless acts of love to her Creator.

20

Her heart was filled with so much love and thanksgiving that Antonietta continued to write letters of love to Jesus. This dedication and love for her closest and dearest friend did not cease when her cancer began to spread throughout her body, and she would write over 100 letters.

Dear Jesus I want to become holy...tell the Holy Spirit that I love Him a lot and that He illuminate me and make me full of His Grace...

"Dear Holy Spirit, you who are the love of the Father and the Son illuminate my heart and soul and bless me...when I make Confirmation you give me all your seven gifts."

Antonietta wrote letters not only to Jesus, but to the Blessed Mother, God the Father, her parents, the Saints, and even to the Holy Spirit! She would tell the Holy Spirit of her desire to receive the Sacrament of Confirmation. Antonietta was too quick for her teacher as she already knew everything about the 7 gifts of the Holy Spirit.

It was May 19, 1937, when her heart's desire was granted and she received the Sacrament of Confirmation !

After her Confirmation, Antonietta's health grew even worse. She became very weak and the pain was severe. Little Antonietta was going to die soon. As the pain increased, so did her strength, love, and joy, because her little heart was always with her sweet Jesus. She was happy to suffer for love of her Beloved Jesus who suffered so much for her.

Dear Crucified Jesus, I want to be on Calvary with You and I suffer with joy because I know how to be on Calvary... Thanks that You have sent me this illness because it's a way to arrive in Paradise

Dear Jesus Eucharist, Today I re-offer my sacrifice of the leg. Dear Jesus, I before everything thank you that you have given the means to come one day closer to You in Paradise. I thank You because you gave us the force to endure with patience our cross. I thank you because in this year I made first Communion and You came to live in my heart...Dear Jesus! It has been several days that I don't see you any more...but You make yourself seen more, because I love you so much! And today I really want to see you!...How painful were these days last year, but I endured all for You dear Jesus!...

So great was her happiness throughout this time that her family wondered if Antonietta was in pain at all. There was always a smile on her face and a light in her eyes.

One day Antonietta told her mother:

"When I suffer immediately I think of Jesus so I don't suffer anymore! It's simple not to suffer: don't think of your pain but think of Jesus, because He suffered so much for us that you won't feel anything yourself."

22

In June Antonietta received the Anointing of the Sick. At first she did not want to, thinking it was too soon, but the priest told her that it would increase grace in her soul. Knowing that grace leads to holiness, Antonietta wanted to receive all the graces that she could, so with joy she said, "Yes, I want it." and stretched out her hands so the priest could anoint them.

The cancer kept spreading through Antonietta's body and her health grew worse and worse.

One day Antonietta's dad asked her, "Do you feel much pain?" Antonietta responded, "Daddy, the pain is like fabric, the stronger it is, the more value it has."

Dear Jesus Crucified, You today died on the Cross to redeem us from sin, I want to adore you and recognize how much you suffered for me ...Dear Jesus You in those three hours of agony when your mom was also present I also want to suffer with the pious women and pour out tears of pain. Dear Jesus I promise you that all the pains that you send me I will offer to You, and every step make it so that it be a little word of love dear Jesus.

Her joy and peace remained and Antonietta knew that her beloved friend Jesus was going to come and bring her to His Great Kingdom of Heaven soon. She was finally going to see not only Jesus, but God the Father, Mother Mary, and all the saints, especially St. Therese, whom she had loved on earth. What a joyful day and greeting that would be !

There was just a little bit of light outside on July 3, 1937 when Jesus came to His little friend to bring her to Paradise where they can always be together. Antonietta's father had just come into her room when he heard his little Nennolina whisper as she looked in front of her,

"Jesus, Mary ...

...Mommy, Daddy"

The little saint then smiled and took one long last breath. She was 6 and a half years old.

Two days later her little white coffin was solemnly processed to the Church for her funeral with a large, emotional crowd accompanying it. On July 5, 1999, 62 years after her funeral, Antonietta's body was moved to a little chapel inside of her beloved Basilica, Santa Croce in Gerusalemme in Rome where she had spent countless hours with Jesus, her everything.

"...I have seen the greatest saints, says God.
Well, I tell you
I have never seen anything finer in the world
Now I tell you, said God,
There is nothing so fine in all the world
Than this child falling asleep saying its prayers
And smiling, slipping into sleep.
Nothing is finer than this small creature falling
asleep in trust...."

– Charles Peguy,
"Mystery of the Holy Innocents"

Antonietta took her last breath on earth but she took her next breath in Heaven. Now she loves Jesus and Mary with all of the love that could not be contained in her little heart while she was on earth. In Heaven, like St. Therese, Antonietta continues her work of bringing souls to God. You can pray to her to help you love God more so that you, too, can become a saint!

After Antonietta died, and seeing the impact she had on so many people, her mother remembered fondly a conversation little Nennolina had with her one day about Heaven.

Nennolina had told her mom,

"I will not amuse myself in Paradise, I will work for souls."

"Really," her mom responded, *"such as St. Therese the Little Flower, who promised a shower of roses...and you, what will you send?"*

Looking straight in front of her, Nennolina replied,

"I'll send a shower of lilies !"

Dear Antonietta,
Send down a shower of lilies upon us and the whole world,
drawing souls back into
the loving and transforming Presence of Jesus Eucharistic.
Help us to burn with that same love that burned in your heart
for our sweet Jesus and Mother Mary, so that we too can love them
as they deserve to be loved, and join you in your work of saving souls.
May Jesus take up His Eucharistic Reign of Love
in my heart and in every heart just as He reigned in yours. Amen,

My Letters to Jesus

Date: _____

Dear Jesus, _____

_____

_____

_____

_____

_____

_____

_____

_____

_____

_____

_____

Date: _____

Dear Jesus,

_____

_____

_____

_____

_____

_____

_____

_____

_____

_____

_____

_____

Date: _____

Dear Jesus, _____

_____

_____

_____

_____

_____

_____

_____

_____

_____

_____

_____

Date: _____

Dear Jesus,
_____
_____
_____
_____
_____
_____
_____
_____
_____
_____
_____
_____
_____

Date: _____

Dear Jesus, _____

_____

_____

_____

_____

_____

_____

_____

_____

_____

_____

_____

_____

Dear Jesus,
_____

_____

_____

_____

_____

_____

_____

_____

_____

_____

_____

_____

Dear Jesus, _____

_____

_____

_____

_____

_____

_____

_____

_____

_____

_____

_____

_____

Dear Jesus,

_____

_____

_____

_____

_____

_____

_____

_____

_____

_____

_____

_____

Date: _____

Dear Jesus, _____

_____

_____

_____

_____

_____

_____

_____

_____

_____

_____

_____

_____

Date: _____

Dear Jesus,

_____

_____

_____

_____

_____

_____

_____

_____

_____

_____

_____

_____

_____

Date: _____

Dear Jesus, _____

_____

_____

_____

_____

_____

_____

_____

_____

_____

_____

_____

_____

Made in the USA
Monee, IL
05 September 2022